The Solar System

Emily Bone

Designed by Helen Edmonds and Will Dawes

Illustrated by Terry Pastor and Tim Haggerty

Solar System consultant: Stuart Atkinson

Reading consultant: Alison Kelly, Principal Lecturer at Roehampton University

Contents

In space

The Earth is a planet. It's a huge, round lump of rock floating in space.

The Earth is one of eight planets that travel around the Sun. The Sun and the planets are called the Solar System.

This is what the Earth looks like from space.

What's out there?

The planets in the Solar System move around the Sun.

The Sun

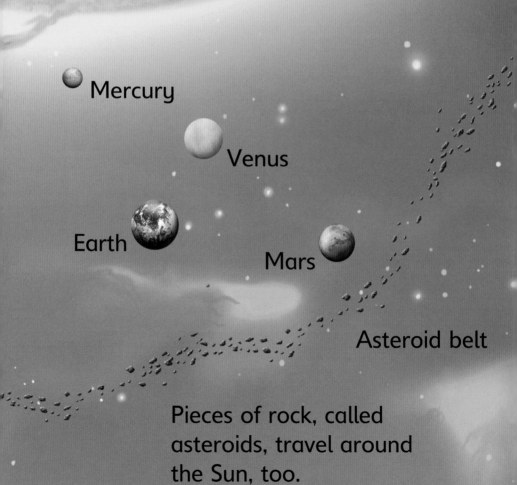

Mercury

Venus

Earth

Mars

Asteroid belt

Pieces of rock, called asteroids, travel around the Sun, too.

The planets are shown close together on these pages. Really, they are very, very far apart.

Saturn

Uranus

Jupiter

Neptune

As well as planets, there are lots of other things that move around the Sun, from specks of dust to 'dwarf planets' such as Pluto.

Pluto

How it started

Scientists think that the Solar System formed millions and millions of years ago.

It began as a huge cloud of gas and dust in space, like this one.

The swirling cloud of gas and dust slowly got thicker and thicker.

Part of the cloud heated up, making a hot ball of gas. This became the Sun.

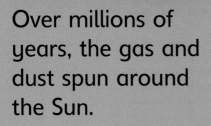

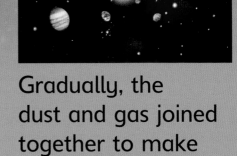

Over millions of years, the gas and dust spun around the Sun.

Gradually, the dust and gas joined together to make the planets.

In the middle

The Sun is a massive ball of
burning gas called a star. It
gives the planets all their
light and heat.

The Sun looks so big
because it is closer
to the Earth than
other stars.

This is what its
surface looks
like close up.

Jets of hot gas
shoot out and fall
back in long loops.

Some parts of the Sun are not as hot as the rest. These are called sunspots.

Huge explosions are known as solar flares.

Never look directly at the Sun. Its light is so strong it could damage your eyes.

Moving planets

Each planet travels along its own path,
or orbit, around the Sun. They take
different lengths of time to move
all of the way around.

Earth takes 365 days
and nights to orbit the
Sun. This is one year.

As the planets travel, they also spin around.
When each planet spins, different parts
have day or night.

Light from the Sun only shines on
one side of the Earth at any time.

This part is dark
because the Sun's
light cannot reach
it. This is night.

The parts facing
the Sun are lit
up. This is the
planet's day.

Mercury

Mercury is the planet closest to the Sun.

Its rocky surface is covered in holes called craters. Most of these were made by rocks crashing into the planet from space.

Fast-moving rocks hit Mercury's surface making deep holes.

Lots of pieces of rock and dust flew up around the holes.

The rock and dust settled in thick layers around the craters.

In this photo,
you can see lots of
round craters on
Mercury's surface.

The surface of Mercury is
more than four times hotter
than boiling water.

Hot planet

Venus is the hottest planet in the Solar System. It is so hot because it is covered in a thick layer of clouds.

This is the surface of Venus. The thick clouds make the sky look orange.

The surface of the planet is hard rock.

The Sun's rays pass through the clouds and the planet's surface warms up.

The clouds stop the heat from escaping so the planet gets hotter and hotter.

Venus is so hot its surface glows in the dark.

Living Earth

The Earth is made of rock and is surrounded by water and gases. It is the only planet where life is known to exist.

The Earth has the right mixture of air, heat and water for things to live.

A layer of gases around Earth gives living things the air they need to breathe.

In this photo, you can see big lakes and high, rocky mountains on Earth's surface.

The Sun warms the planet. Plants grow in sunlight, making food for animals.

More than half of the Earth is covered in water. Everything needs water to live.

Bright at night

The Moon is a big, round lump of rock that moves around the Earth. It is the brightest thing you can see in the night sky.

There are millions of craters on the Moon. In this photo, the biggest craters look like dark patches.

As the Moon moves, the Sun lights up different parts of its surface. This is why the Moon seems to change shape.

When the side facing Earth is lit up, you can see the Moon as a bright circle.

Sometimes, you can only see part of the side that is lit by the Sun.

When the Sun shines behind the Moon you can't see the bright side, so it looks dark.

In 1969, astronauts landed on the Moon in a spacecraft.

The red planet

Mars is a cold and rocky planet. Its surface is covered in red dust. Scientists have sent vehicles called rovers to Mars to take photos of the surface.

A rover was packed inside a spacecraft and flown from Earth to Mars.

Air bags protected the spacecraft as it landed on the planet's surface.

This is a photo of Mars' surface, taken by a rover.

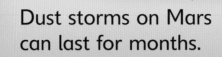

Dust storms on Mars
can last for months.

The spacecraft
opened up and
scientists sent signals
to drive the rover out.

The rover drove
around, sending
information back to
scientists on Earth.

Gas giant

Jupiter is the biggest planet in the Solar System. It is a huge, round mass made mostly from gases.

The stripes you can see here are bands of different gases.

Jupiter has over 60 moons moving around it.
All the moons are made of rock and ice.

 Thebe is not round like most moons.
Its surface is covered in huge craters.

The rocky surface of Europa
is completely covered in a
layer of ice.

Ganymede is the biggest
moon in the Solar System.
It is bigger than Mercury.

There is a huge storm on
Jupiter that has been raging for
thousands of years.

Ringed planet

Saturn is a huge planet made mostly of gases. It has millions of pieces of rock and ice moving around it. From far away, these look like solid rings.

This photo was taken from a spacecraft that scientists sent to fly around Saturn.

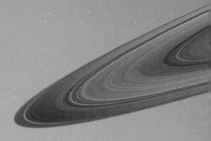

In 1997, a rocket took off from Earth. It was controlled by computers.

When the rocket was far above the Earth, a probe flew away from it.

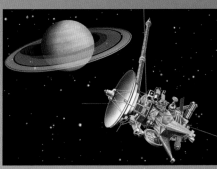

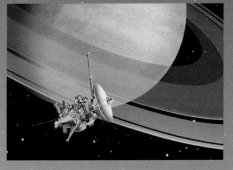

The probe reached
Saturn and started
to fly around and
around the planet.

It sent close-up
pictures of Saturn
and its rings back
to Earth.

Distant planets

Uranus and Neptune are huge gas planets.

This is Uranus. It has faint rings around it made from millions of specks of dust.

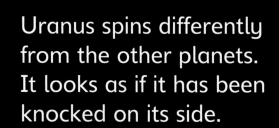

Uranus spins differently from the other planets. It looks as if it has been knocked on its side.

Neptune is a very cold and stormy planet. This dark blue swirl is a storm raging on the planet.

Beyond Neptune, there is a dwarf planet called Pluto. Experts used to think it was a planet but they've changed their minds.

Exploring the sky

Scientists find out about the Solar System by using huge telescopes that let them see things that are very far away.

The telescopes shown here are in Hawaii, U.S.A. They use big, curved mirrors to make things that are far away look a lot bigger.

There are some telescopes that travel around the Earth in space.

1. Scientists on Earth send signals to point the telescope at a planet.

2. The telescope takes pictures of the planet and stores them in a computer.

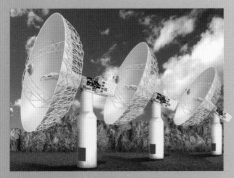

3. The computer sends the pictures as signals to huge radio dishes on Earth.

4. The information is sent to computers that turn them into pictures of the planet.

Glossary

Here are some of the words in this book you might not know. This page tells you what they mean.

 planet - a huge mass of rock or gas in space that moves around the Sun.

 asteroid - a lump of rock that moves around the Sun.

 orbit - the path of something as it goes around something else.

 crater - a round hole on a planet or moon made by a rock crashing into it.

 rover - a computer-controlled vehicle that drives across a planet.

 probe - a computer-controlled spacecraft sent to explore space.

 telescope - something that makes things that are far away look bigger.

Websites to visit

You can visit exciting websites to find out more about the Solar System.

To visit these websites, go to the Usborne Quicklinks Website at **www.usborne-quicklinks.com** Read the internet safety guidelines, and then type the keywords "**beginners solar system**".

The websites are regularly reviewed and the links in Usborne Quicklinks are updated. However, Usborne Publishing is not responsible, and does not accept liability, for the content or availability of any website other than its own. We recommend that children are supervised while on the internet.

This is the International Space Station. Scientists live on it and do experiments to find out more about space.

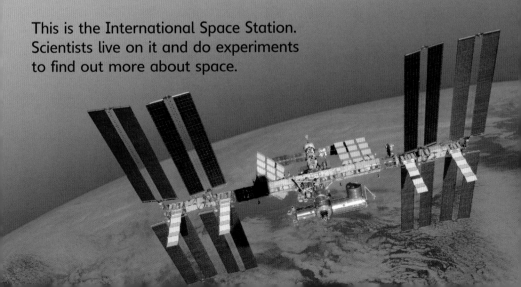

Index

Acknowledgements

Photographic manipulation by John Russell

Photo credits
The publishers are grateful to the following for permission to reproduce material:
© Chris Knorr/Design Pics Inc./Corbis **28**; © Design Pics Inc./Photolibrary **18** (Corey Hochachka);
© Detlev van Ravensway/Science Photo Library **cover background**; © ESA/NASA/SOHO **08-09**;
© Gavin Hellier/Robert Harding **16-17**; © Mark Garlick/Science Photo Library **27**; © NASA **cover, 22, 31**;
© NASA Goddard Space Flight Center (NASA-GSFC) **02-03**; © NASA Jet Propulsion Laboratory (NASA-JPL)
13, 14-15, 26; © NASA/JPL-Caltech **24-25 background;** © NASA/JPL-Caltech/Cornell **20-21**; © NASA/JPL-
Caltech/L. Allen (Harvard-Smithsonian CfA) **06-07**; © NASA/JPL/Cornell University **23**; © NASA/JPL/DLR **23**;
© NASA/JPL/Space Science Institute cover, **24-25**; © Roger Ressmeyer/CORBIS **01**.

Every effort has been made to trace and acknowledge ownership of copyright. If any rights have
been omitted, the publishers offer to rectify this in any subsequent editions following notification.